DISABILITY AND THE DISABLED –ISSUES, LAWS AND PROGRAMS

HUMAN MOTOR DEVELOPMENT IN INDIVIDUALS WITH AND WITHOUT DISABILITIES

DISABILITY AND THE DISABLED –ISSUES, LAWS AND PROGRAMS

Additional books in this series can be found on Nova's website at:

https://www.novapublishers.com/catalog/index.php?cPath=23_29&seriesp=Disability+and+the+Disabled-Issues%2C+Laws+and+Programs

Additional E-books can be found on Nova's website at:

https://www.novapublishers.com/catalog/index.php?cPath=23_29&seriespe=Disability+and+the+Disabled-Issues%2C+Laws+and+Programs

DISABILITY AND THE DISABLED – ISSUES, LAWS AND PROGRAMS

HUMAN MOTOR DEVELOPMENT IN INDIVIDUALS WITH AND WITHOUT DISABILITIES

V. GREGORY PAYNE
JIN H. YAN
AND
MARTIN BLOCK

Nova Science Publishers, Inc.
New York

Copyright © 2010 by Nova Science Publishers, Inc.

All rights reserved. No part of this book may be reproduced, stored in a retrieval system or transmitted in any form or by any means: electronic, electrostatic, magnetic, tape, mechanical photocopying, recording or otherwise without the written permission of the Publisher.

For permission to use material from this book please contact us:
Telephone 631-231-7269; Fax 631-231-8175
Web Site: http://www.novapublishers.com

NOTICE TO THE READER

The Publisher has taken reasonable care in the preparation of this book, but makes no expressed or implied warranty of any kind and assumes no responsibility for any errors or omissions. No liability is assumed for incidental or consequential damages in connection with or arising out of information contained in this book. The Publisher shall not be liable for any special, consequential, or exemplary damages resulting, in whole or in part, from the readers' use of, or reliance upon, this material. Any parts of this book based on government reports are so indicated and copyright is claimed for those parts to the extent applicable to compilations of such works.

Independent verification should be sought for any data, advice or recommendations contained in this book. In addition, no responsibility is assumed by the publisher for any injury and/or damage to persons or property arising from any methods, products, instructions, ideas or otherwise contained in this publication.

This publication is designed to provide accurate and authoritative information with regard to the subject matter covered herein. It is sold with the clear understanding that the Publisher is not engaged in rendering legal or any other professional services. If legal or any other expert assistance is required, the services of a competent person should be sought. FROM A DECLARATION OF PARTICIPANTS JOINTLY ADOPTED BY A COMMITTEE OF THE AMERICAN BAR ASSOCIATION AND A COMMITTEE OF PUBLISHERS.

LIBRARY OF CONGRESS CATALOGING-IN-PUBLICATION DATA

Aviailable upon request

ISBN 978-1-61668-235-4

Published by Nova Science Publishers, Inc. ✢ *New York*

CONTENTS

Introduction		i
Chapter 1	The Significance of the Study of Human Motor Development	1
Chapter 2	Understanding Human Motor Development: The Mountain Metaphor	3
Chapter 3	Unique Development Considerations for Children with Various Disabilities	17
Hearing Loss Table		41
Summary and Conclusions		43
References		45
Index		51

INTRODUCTION

We have all held a newborn with her head gently cupped in our hand to help maintain the head's upright position. Even a month or so after birth, many babies may need that supporting hand to compensate for the lack of muscle strength and control of their necks. However, by the second month of post birth life, babies have typically gained enough neck strength to raise and hold their heads upright. Many experts consider this to be the first major motor milestone of motor development in infancy. And, by two or three months of life, infants can normally hold their heads up and even turn them from side to side when lying on the floor in a prone position (Frankenburg, Dodds, Fandal, Kazuk, & Cohrs, 1992). By five months of life, the babies can raise their heads when in a supine position on the floor. This common and expected progression in controlling the head is just one example of early human motor development.

Human motor performance is one of the fundamental aspects of the sensory-motor system. Many questions appeal to researchers in the field of movement science and other areas such as neuroscience, psychology, physiology, education, pediatrics, and geriatrics. For example, how do humans learn and control movements? Considering that humans improve motor performance in childhood as a function of enriched experiences or maturation, developmental studies on motor performance inform our understanding of perceptual-motor skills (Thomas, Yan, & Stelmach, 2000; Yan, Thomas, Stelmach, & Thomas, 2000; Zelazo, Craik, & Booth, 2004). A developmental approach can answer questions like why children exhibit certain consistent motor behavior. When and how do these motor behaviors begin? Are these behaviors learned behaviors or naturally developed? A better understanding of these questions has critical implications.

The purpose of this chapter is to discuss key concepts related to human motor development, especially as they pertain to childhood, and examine the application of this information in populations of children with and without disabilities. By definition, **human motor development is "the changes in human movement behavior over the lifespan, the processes that underlie these changes and the factors that affect them"** (Payne & Isaacs, 2008, p. 3). It is a process that we all undergo as a part of the gradually evolving maturation from inception through death, the qualitative change in our function that accompanies getting older. Because it is such a subtle and gradually emerging process, motor development often goes unnoticed and unappreciated. However, as you will see throughout this chapter, it is a critical process that impacts, and is impacted, by all other aspects of human development – physical, social-emotional, and intellectual development. It is a process that is integral to achieving our full maturity and potential as human beings.

Chapter 1

THE SIGNIFICANCE OF THE STUDY OF HUMAN MOTOR DEVELOPMENT

Knowing and understanding the sequences of change in our motor development and the factors that affect these changes can be extremely important in education. Physical education teachers, for example, need to have an understanding of what children have done, what they are capable of doing, and what the likely next step in their development might be to be able to devise student learning outcomes for their classes as well as develop appropriate lesson plans. Without a thorough understanding of their students' motor development, creating developmentally appropriate lesson plans is difficult. Lessons are likely to be too simple and boring for their students or too difficult and frustrating. In short, teaching practices should be developmentally appropriate. According to the National Association for the Education of Young Children (NAEYC), this means that "Programs should be tailored to meet the needs of children rather than expecting the children to adapt to the demands of specific programs" (Bredekamp & Copple, 1997, p.1). The NAEYC suggests that developmentally appropriate includes two related dimensions, age appropriate and individual appropriate. Age appropriate relates to the importance of being knowledgeable of the relatively predictable growth and development sequences through which most children pass. These sequences are integral to the creation of viable learning opportunities for children. Though most children pass through these predictable sequences, they are still unique as they proceed through varying rates and patterns of development with their individual modes of learning, personalities, and out-of-school environments. These factors are critical to the term individual appropriateness and are also important considerations when creating educational experiences for young children.

Motor development is assumed to follow a specific or universal order, therefore, can be used in movement education or as a diagnostic tool. For instance, in terms of evaluating motor skill development, a teacher can report an individual's performance relative to that of other students of the same age, gender, or skill level or class (norm-referenced evaluation). On the other hand, a coach or teacher can evaluate someone's performance relative to a criterion or cutoff score that the coach or teacher wants the students to achieve (criterion-based evaluation). In choosing a particular approach to evaluate motor development in children, an important concern is whether it is developmentally appropriate. Motor development is age-related, not age-dependent. It is, therefore, necessary to evaluate motor performance of an individual or a group of individuals by comparing with others in the same age group (normative). However, it is equally important to consider individual differences in motor development and performance, because biological and environmental factors play a role in the development. Understanding motor development will allow a teacher or coach to know why a student is more or less movement proficient than his or her age-peers in motor performance. Understanding these developmental differences facilitates decision making related to enhancing motor ability in children.

Chapter 2

UNDERSTANDING HUMAN MOTOR DEVELOPMENT: THE MOUNTAIN METAPHOR

To describe the complexities of human motor development in one chapter is a considerable challenge. Some might argue that a book would be insufficient. However, ways have been devised to help explain some of the most important aspects of human motor development in a more simplified, easily understandable, form. Clark and Metcalfe, 2002), for example, have proposed a "Mountain of Motor Development" as a metaphor for "the big picture" of the changes in human movement throughout life. This metaphor "emphasizes the cumulative, sequential, and interactive nature of motor skill development as an emergent product of lifelong changes within a multitude of constraints on our behavior" (p. 163). According to Clark and Metcalfe, previous metaphors devised in the examination of human motor development have focused on the product(s) of human movement where an emphasis was placed on describing the observed movement. Others have placed an emphasis on the process of the movement as they attempted to interpret the underlying explanations for the movement change. Clark and Metcalfe argue an opt for what they call an integrated metaphor where both the products and processes of movement are considered. It encompasses "periods" that one would pass through as they "climb the mountain" of life. Clark and Metcalfe believe their metaphor symbolizes the time it takes to learn the motor skills of life while showing the sequential nature and cumulative effect of the "climb." In addition, through their metaphor, these authors seek to symbolize the significant impact of factors like instruction, practice, and learning as well as inherent individual differences. Clark and Metcalfe also believe that human motor development is impacted by many constraints, factors that confine, or variously affect the way that we eventually move. These constraints are continually changing, thus having a variable impact on individual motor skill acquisition. They arise from the performer, the performer's environment, or may be related to the task in question. And, of course, we must also consider the interaction between all of these constraints and their relative effect on motor skill performance. Imagine, for example, someone climbing the metaphorical mountain. The climber is affected by his or her own personal strengths or limitations (e.g., endurance, strength, reach, motivation) the nature of the mountain (steep, high, number of handholds, number of passages), weather conditions (e.g., cold, icy, windy), and, of course, the interaction of all of these factors at any one time.

To illustrate the so-called products of motor development, Clark and Metcalfe also integrate six periods of motor development into their metaphor, the mountain. These periods begin during the prenatal state and are referred to as the reflexive, preadapted, fundamental patterns, context-specific, skillful, and compensation periods. The authors note that progression up the mountain is very individual with "climbers" accumulating skill in a sequential process as they go higher. Each period provides the "climber" with necessary prerequisites to assist the progression to the next period.

The journey up the hill begins during prenatal life when the body is forming. Immediately, constraints begin to impact development. For example, the fetus is affected by parental factors that may have far-reaching and long-term effects on the baby. For example, did the mother eat a healthy diet, exercise, smoke, drink excessive amounts of alcohol, experience excess stress, or contract a disease that could affect the fetus? The individual is also a product of their genetic makeup. All of these factors, and many more, will affect the climb up the mountain. Of course, the changing terrain encountered once the climb begins is symbolic of the varying paths we all take as we pass through life.

REFLEXIVE PERIOD

Clark and Metcalfe's first period, the Reflexive Period, generally exists for several weeks pre- birth and for a variable period of time after we are born. This period is particularly important as the reflexive movement exhibited in this period is important for sustaining survival while enabling beginning interactions with the surrounding world. The first year or year and a half of life is often referred to as infancy. The term infancy literally refers to the lack of speech that is one of the prime characteristics of this time of life (Piek, 2006). During the early weeks and months of infancy, one of the most fascinating human movement forms is prevalent. Infant reflexes are "involuntary movements that are generally elicited by an external stimulus specific to that particular reflex..." (Piek, 2006; p. 17). They are characterized by being stereotypical and subcortical. Stereotypical implies that they occur virtually the same each time they are elicited. For example, the well known palmar grasp reflex normally appears from slightly before birth to about four months of age. A stroke of the infant's palm will elicit a closing of the four fingers; usually the thumb is not involved. Each time the hand is stimulated, the reaction is virtually the same. Similarly, the sucking reflex is elicited upon a tactile stimulation of the baby's lips; the baby responds by a sucking action. Subcortical implies that the higher brain centers like the motor cortex are relatively uninvolved in the production of the movement. Thus, infant reflexes do not appear to be learned. Rather, they seem to be "prewired" in the normal infant. When a stimulus is applied, like the stroke of the hand, an impulse is sent to through the central nervous system to the lower brain or brain stem. Though the process is far from understood, we believe that the impulse is processed and sent back to the hand where a "close the hand" message is delivered (Payne & Isaacs, 2008).

Another very different example of an infant reflex is the labyrinthine reflex. This reflex can normally be elicited from approximately two to twelve months. It is elicited by holding the infant upright. As the baby is tipped to one side or the other, the head responds by tilting in the opposite direction. If the baby is tipped to the front or back, the head will respond by tilting backwards or forwards. Though little evidence is available to support the assertion, one might suspect that this reflex is primary in the establishment of eventual upright sitting and standing posture.

Because there are many infant reflexes, they have been categorized into the primitive and the postural types. The primitive reflexes are those which are believed to protect and nourish us when we are incapable of doing that for ourselves. Note, the sucking reflex mentioned above would be considered a primitive reflex, because of the role it plays in ingesting nourishment. The postural reflexes are those that are believed to play a role in the development of more advanced voluntary movement, learned movement that that is created as a result of an impulse from higher brain centers. An example of a postural reflex is the stepping or walking reflex. This reflex can be elicited by holding a baby upright with the floor or a tabletop applying a force to the bottoms of the feet. This stimulus will create an alternate stepping action of the legs that gives the appearance of a surprisingly mature walking action of the legs.

The exact relationship of the postural reflexes to ensuing voluntary movements like reaching, grasping, sitting, standing, or even walking, is unknown. However, researchers have examined the effects of manipulation of certain reflexes on the time of appearance of certain voluntary movements. One of the best examples of this type of research was conducted by Zelazo and associates (1993). In this classis research, the researchers repeatedly stimulated the stepping reflex with six-week-old infants. Compared to a control group, these infants were found to voluntarily step more on their own. **The researchers speculated that the regular "practice" of the research may have enhanced the infant's equilibrium** and strength of the stepping related muscles prompting the baby to more voluntary attempts at stepping.

In normal, healthy babies infant reflexes can be seen starting at birth and lasting past the first birthday. For example, the search or rooting reflex is typically present at birth. **This reflex can be elicited by stroking the baby's cheek to the right or left of the mouth.** The baby will turn the head toward the side of the stimulated cheek. This is a primitive reflex that is nourishment related. **This reflex helps the baby locate the mother's nipple for sustenance.** Once the nipple is located, the lips are stimulated to begin the sucking reflex for ingestion of breast milk. Like the search reflex, the sucking reflex is present at birth. However, both reflexes will subside at around three months of age.

The time of appearance of infant reflexes is somewhat variable individually, however, the reflexes are predictable enough to be used in pediatric diagnosis where they can be reasonably accurate predictors of a **baby's neurological maturity (Malina, Bouchard, & Bar-Or, 2004).** In such tests, pediatricians will look for significant deviations in the time of appearance, the strength, or the symmetry. Occasionally, a reflex may not appear at all. This, too, may be an indicator of a neurological impairment. Many of the infant reflexes are symmetrical in appearance. For example, children with cerebral palsy (a motor impairment rooted in early damage to the brain) often continue to demonstrate primitive reflexes such as the startle, grasping, and asymmetrically tonic neck reflex well into early childhood and even into their teens. The persistence of primitive reflexes into early childhood is an indication of neurological impairment, and additional testing should be requested (Zafeiriou, 2004).

While infant reflexes are a dominant form of movement over the first few weeks of life, the presence and significance of these movements gradually diminishes across the first year of life. Infant reflexes are gradually over-ridden or replaced by movements that are under voluntary control. This process gradually evolves until just after the first year of life when we are no longer able to elicit most of the infant reflexes. Despite the disappearance of these reactions, a number of reflexes remain and will be maintained throughout life in normal and healthy individuals. These reflexes, however, are not considered infant reflexes, because they are normal and expected beyond infancy. Examples of such lifelong reflexes are the knee jerk where the patellar tendon is abruptly tapped eliciting a sudden jerk of the leg into a partial extension at the knee.

PREADAPTED PERIOD

Clark and Metcalfe's second period of their Mountain of Motor Development is characterized by the gradual "disappearance or inhibition" of the infant reflexes. During this period of time, voluntary movement becomes increasingly prevalent. By voluntary movement, we refer to movement that is intentionally, often consciously, initiated by the individual. This is in contrast to reflexive movement that is elicited by an external stimulus causing the individual to move. Clark and Metcalfe chose the term Pre-adapted Period to reflect the "progressive mastery of the body in a gravitational environment" (Clark and Metcalfe, 2002; p. 175). Clearly, the individual's genetic structure and environment create an extensive repertoire of possibilities for movement. Within that interaction, Clark and Metcalfe believe that the goal of this period of development is the achievement of an increased level of functional independence. This ranges from increased independence in feeding to exploring one's own environment via independent locomotion to increasing pursuit of social interactions as a result of the evolving independence of movement (e.g., crawling, walking).

Movements in this period of development are often divided into three categories, stability, manipulation, and locomotion (Gallahue & Ozmun, 2006). Stability involves those movements that enable us to control the body or place it in the desired position. Examples would include head control, rolling from front to back or back to front, sitting, and even standing. Manipulation involves the use of the hands and arms and locomotion involves the movement from one point in space to another (e.g., crawling, walking).

Though all of these movements are critical to our existence and are clear examples of our developing movement, space limits our discussion of all of them. We will, however, focus on crawling as one example of the changes in movement behavior during this Pre-adaptive Period. Because the terms creeping and crawling are not consistently used and interpreted, some explanation is required. For our purposes, crawling is considered the less mature movement form that is often characterized by a pre-creeping movement that is highly variable, somewhat inefficient, usually low to the ground, and intending to propel the body forward. Creeping is the more mature locomotor pattern that generally follows by around 7 to 8 months of age. It is characterized by a higher, more efficient and upright, hand and knee form of locomotion with the torso elevated of the floor (Payne & Isaacs, 2008).

Adolph, Vereijken, and Denny (1998) studied 28 babies starting to crawl until they began to walk. The researchers were particularly interested in the **effects of the baby's age**, their body dimensions, and their previous experiences on crawling development. Generally, sequential and continuous improvement was seen in the way the babies crawled and how quickly they crawled. Despite many similarities in the way the babies crawled, there were also many differences demonstrating the individual variability in motor development at this time of life. Some of the babies skipped characteristics of crawling development that were quite common in others. One example was crawling on the belly or low-crawling where nearly half of the babies were **found to "skip" this piece of the developmental progression**. Characteristics that were encountered regularly included elevating the head and chest from the ground, pulling forward while the lower torso was still in contact with the supporting surface, and rocking rhythmically while in the crawling position. The progression of overall crawling development did not seem to be absolute, but rather, somewhat variable from baby to baby as many different crawling positions were exhibited. The earliest form of crawling was characterized by dragging the lower torso on the floor. Experience was clearly a factor as those babies with more exposure to crawling became more efficient and faster crawlers at an earlier age. Size was also a factor as smaller, leaner babies were found to crawl earlier than larger babies. Finally, hands and knees creeping (locomoting with the torso elevated off the floor on the hands and knees) was typically the final locomotor milestone before the onset of walking (Adolph, Vereijken, & Denny, 1998).

FUNDAMENTAL PATTERNS PERIOD

During the Fundamental Patterns Period of the Mountain, the young mover uses existing skill to advance to a level of movement that is often considered the base of many future movement skills. This period is formulated during infancy, but is often considered to last until approximately seven years of life (Clark & Metcalfe, 2002). At that time, these movements will gradually be applied to specific movement situations, like sports. Thus, these movements are often referred to as the "building blocks" of more context specific movements of later life (Clark & Metcalfe, p. 176; Payne & Isaacs, p.300). Without a solid base of ability in these fundamental movements, achieving a mature level of movement ability in the more complex and combined movements associated with later life will become more difficult or impossible to achieve. As in the previous periods of development, substantial differences may be noted in the skill levels of children based on their previous opportunity, experience, instruction, and practice of the skill in question.

The fundamental movements, or motor patterns, can be organized in several ways. Payne & Isaacs (2008) make reference to two types of fundamental movements: the fundamental locomotion skills and the fundamental object control skills. While locomotion, moving from one point in space to another (e.g., walking) really began in earlier periods of the mountain, it is during this time that real progress is typically noted, even to the extent of seeing nearly adult like skill evolving in many aspects of the child's ability in the fundamental locomotion skills like walking, running, jumping, hopping, leaping, skipping, and galloping. In addition, children commonly increase their interaction with objects (e.g., balls, rackets, bats) in their environment as they develop fundamental object control skills like throwing, catching, ball bouncing, kicking, and striking.

Research has indicated that fairly predictable development sequences exist in the fundamental movements (Roberton & Halverson, 1984). Though space will not allow for an examination of all of the fundamental movements, an examination of the relatively predictable sequences for one pattern will be useful as an example. Researchers (Roberton, 1983; Seefeldt, Reuschlein, and Vogel, 1972) have hypothesized that initial efforts to run are characterized by relatively flat-footed running as the feet generally contact the supporting surface with the entire foot. The legs are often abducted (i.e. swung out to the side) in immature runners as the leg recovers to the front position. Toes are often pointed out slightly and the angle (bend at the knee) of the recovering leg often exceeds ninety degrees during the recovery. In other words, the legs stay relatively straight compared to more mature runners. The stride is relatively short and inconsistent in both length and landing position. The arms are typically held in a high guard position and make little contribution to generating momentum for the run. They are held above the shoulders in a "high guard" position (Payne & Isaacs, 2008).

Gradually, with maturity, instruction, experience, and practice, the running pattern becomes more mature. This is illustrated by a more noticeable bend in the recovering leg, the amount of out-toeing is reduced, and the arms begin to lower into a position where they can assist in the generation of force for the run. The decreasing amount of abduction of the recovering leg is also a common characteristic of increasing maturity in the running pattern. With the onset of these more mature characteristics, we also note an increase flight time during the run. Flight time is the period in which no body part is touching the ground, one foot has just pushed off, but the opposite foot has not yet contacted the supporting surface. This is most likely a function of both the maturation of the movement technique as well as the child's increasing strength and power.

As the arms lower, the immature runner may exhibit a rotation of the upper body, or trunk, and a crossing of the body's midline with the slightly flexed arms as they swing through in the forward position. Also, noticeable when viewed from the rear, and perhaps a reaction to the upper body rotation, is the foot crossing the midline when behind the body. The stride gradually elongates and becomes more consistent in both length and foot placement.

A mature runner will assume a greater forward inclination and no longer exhibit the flat-footed characteristics described earlier. Typically, the heal of toe will make initial contact as the leg swings more directly straight forward and back with a significant flexion in each leg as it swings through in both the front and rear positions. However, once the rear leg reaches the full push-off position it will be nearing full extension in the mature runner. The amount of upper body rotation will diminish with the arms now swinging straight forward and straight back (sagittal plane) in a flexed position. The arms, swinging in opposition to each other, and in opposition to the same-side leg, drive through to provide additional force to achieve greater velocity in the run. Similarly, the legs will no longer cross the midline as they, too, swing straight forward and back with a minimum of excess motion (Payne & Isaacs, 2008).

Research has found that sixty percent of boys were able to perform at a mature level by four years of age. Sixty percent of girls were able to perform at a mature level by slightly more than five years of age (Seefeldt & Haubenstricker, 1982). Note, however, that these percentages were determined using a "total-body" assessment of movement. In other words, the observer makes an overall assessment of the general level of maturity of all aspects of the performer's movement. While this is a relatively simple and useful method of assessing the development of fundamental movement, it may not convey a completely accurate analysis of movement. This is because a child will often exhibit relatively mature characteristics in one aspect of the fundamental movement, like running, while others remain relatively immature. For example, a child may have a relatively mature arm action with the arms in the lowered position, flexed at nearly a ninety degree angle, and swinging through in opposition to the leg on the same side of the body. At the same time, however, the leg action may be characterized by a lack of leg flexion, a bent leg at push-off, and a slight abduction of the legs as they swing through – all relatively immature characteristics. For this reason, fundamental movement is often assessed by a "component" approach where individual assessment is made of the specific body parts involved in the movement. While this system is generally believed to provide more accurate information, it is less administratively efficient for many practitioners in a teaching setting.

Regardless of which assessment technique is employed, knowledge of the expected developmental trends in movements like running can be invaluable in making instructional decisions related to the student's level of maturity in a given movement pattern, assessing when a child might be able to achieve maturity in a given movement patterns, and designing educational programs to assist children in attaining higher levels of maturity in a given movement pattern. Thus, knowledge of motor development can yield informed decisions related to the education of children in physical education, sports, recreational, and fitness activities.

CONTEXT SPECIFIC PERIOD

The Context Specific Period of the Mountain metaphor builds off of the skills developed in the previous period. The fundamental movement patterns (e.g., running, jumping, throwing, catching, kicking) are honed as the child's skill level improves. The mover gradually develops an ability to adapt these movements to new and different situations where the constraints may demand increased ability at adapting the movement to the demands of the movement setting. Achieving this level of ability in the fundamental movements varies widely from child to child. However, according to Clark and Metcalfe (2002), achieving this period of the Mountain could occur as early as four years of age in rare cases. More commonly, however, it would be expected closer to seven years of age. Nevertheless, more mature performers may also find themselves at this point on the Mountain, or below. For example, a young adult may decide to take-up tennis with little or no previous experience. Initially, as they begin to develop a more mature striking pattern (i.e., forehand, backhand, or serve), they may find themselves on the Fundamental Patterns Period of the Mountain working their way up to the Context Specific Period. This is a clear indicator that one's status on the Mountain is not just age related. It reflects much more than how much time has been spent "climbing." It is also affected by the array of one's unique life experiences like where and how they are raised. For example, we often find that children raised near a beach or an ocean may develop skills differently that those who are not. Aquatic activities like swimming, diving, surfing, or beach volleyball may be prevalent. In addition, certain geographic areas are more culturally predisposed to certain activities. For example, a child raised in the northeastern part of the United States would be more likely to play Lacrosse that a child raised in the Western or Southern United States where that sport is not as common.

As children "climb" up into this period of development, they will begin to use their fundamental movement abilities in more sophisticated ways. They will simultaneously combine one fundamental movement with another, or several others, while performing the movement in the face of increasing movement demands. They may begin to combine throwing with running as required in basketball or football, or catching while funning as required in baseball. They may seek to achieve greater accuracy or speed in the movement, or perform the movement with many more constraints than previously imagined. An example would be the progression from simply dribbling a basketball while standing to dribble the ball while running, even weaving, through a series of defenders on the basketball court. Obviously, this involves increasing perceptual-cognitive demands. The performer must more fully understand the constraints of the surrounding situation to achieve more success motorically. For example, when dribbling the ball down court, having a greater understanding of the possible defensive responses of the opposing team may signal a need to dribble right or left, or faster or slower.

Clark and Metcalfe believe that this period of time is particularly important, because one's level of success and feelings of competence in the performance of movements will impact future decisions governing their participation. Having a more fully developed skill level in the fundamental movements is integral to this success (Clark and Metcalfe, 2002).

SKILLFUL PERIOD

Not everyone will achieve this level of the Mountain, and this period is rarely achieved by a child. However, for many with sufficient instruction, practice, experience, and opportunity, an individual can climb from the Context-specific period of the Mountain to the Skillful Period. Skillful implies that a mover can perform with such a high level of ability that movement is performed confidently with the potential to integrate movements into situations requiring strategic analysis to enhance performance. Thus, like in the Context-specific Period, the cognitive component of movement is intertwined with the level of movement performance.

Interestingly, this period of the Mountain can be attained for one or more movement skills. In fact, some performers may even become quite skillful in many, though no one attains this level in most or all movement skills. This level of skill is rarely attained without considerable effort on the part of the performer and many people may never find the need or desire to achieve this level of skill. Seeking proper instruction or coaching and practicing that which has been taught are integral to skillful movement. Being motivated to achieve such a level is also critical. This suggests that the performer is in an environment where these opportunities are available. It may include having parents who are encouraging, friends who are supportive, and the surrounding culture that provides adequate incentive to improve. Of course, it also requires that inherent physical, cognitive, emotional, and motor capabilities are present. For example, performing a skilled back hand spring in gymnastics may not be possible if the performer lacks adequate strength, power, and agility to execute the movement. For some, even with instruction and practice, inherent characteristics may be too limiting to allow execution of the movement. That back handspring, for example, may be much more difficult, even impossible, for someone who is exceptionally tall, or dunking a basketball may be unachievable for someone who is exceptionally short regardless of their superior jumping ability.

According to Clark and Metcalfe (2002), this period of the Mountain often coincides with the onset of the adolescent growth spurt at puberty, though many exceptions exist. We have all seen evidence of elite level performers, like swimmers, tennis players, or gymnasts who have achieved superior levels of skill at very young ages. Similarly, many individuals may never be motivated to achieve such a level of skill until much later in life, even as late as middle adulthood or beyond. For some, this level of skill will simply never be achieved. However, when this level of expertise is achieved, it generally requires time, considerable practice, appropriate instruction, and the appropriate interaction of the performer's own biological characteristics with the surrounding environment. For that reason, exceptionally high levels of skill, expertise, often may not be achieved until early adulthood.

COMPENSATION PERIOD

Clark and Metcalfe's final period of the Mountain is referred to as the Compensation period (2002) where motor development continues to emerge. Our major emphasis in this paper is to provide an overview of movement during childhood. This period of the mountain is generally seen in the adult years. Nevertheless, because it is the last period of the metaphor, a brief examination of the major characteristics of the period is in order. As the name implies, compensation is integral to this period of development. According to the authors, this indicates that the human system may be interacting in a substandard way requiring adaptations for the movement in question to be performed. These adaptations may be necessary as a result of physical injury or as a function of the normal aging process. For example, a spinal cord injury may require considerable adjustments to re-learn sitting, standing, or walking. In severe cases, these behaviors may not be possible, so adaptations may focus on the use of the hands and arms in reaching and grasping movements. Similarly, children born with disabilities must learn to compensate for the disabilities. A child who is born with a visual impairment learns how to move relying on visual and tactile cues rather than visual cues, and a child born without legs learns to walk and run with prosthetics and crutches or perhaps learns to move and play sports using a wheelchair.

In the case of older performers, a gradual slowing with age, reduced strength or flexibility may similarly require adaptations to the way movements are performed, or decision as to which movements may no longer be possible. Regardless of whether the compensations are injury or age related, the system must reorganize or shift to accommodate a changing movement repertoire. Generally, this period involves the latter part of life when motor development is experienced or seen as a decline or regression occurring as the physical characteristics (e.g., strength, endurance, speed of movement). More positively, we can view this time of life as an adaptation or series of adjustments to the ever changing system that governs of motor development. In addition, considerable evidence points to the dramatic positive effect of physical activity and exercise on overcoming the rate of decline of the physiological systems that influence our motor development (Clark & Metcalfe, 2002). Nevertheless, regardless of the activity level one maintains, the regressive effects of the aging process are inevitable.

Chapter 3

UNIQUE DEVELOPMENT CONSIDERATIONS FOR CHILDREN WITH VARIOUS DISABILITIES

The previous discussion of the Mountain of Motor Development outlined a typical course of development seen in most children without disabilities. However, there are certain types of disabilities that can affect how quickly children progress up the mountain and how high they progress up the mountain. For example, children with Down syndrome (a genetic cause of intellectual disabilities) are often delayed in walking by more than a year compared to children without intellectual disabilities, and some children with Down syndrome may never reach the context-specific period of motor development. The sections describe some of the more common types of developmental disabilities and how these disabilities can impact normal motor development. Note that due to space constraints and the diversity of characteristics children with physical disabilities were not included in this discussion.

CHILDREN WITH INTELLECTUAL DISABILITIES

The term intellectual disability (ID) is the new preferred term for what had been referred to as mental retardation (Schalock et al., 2007). The American Association for Intellectual and Developmental Disabilities (AAIDD) produced the definitive definition of ID for several decades now. The most recent definition is: "An intellectual disability is a disability characterized by significant limitations both in intellectual functioning and in adaptive behavior as expressed in conceptual, social, and practical adaptive skills. This disability originates before the age of 18" (Luckasson et al., 2002, p. 1). A significant limitation in intellectual functioning refers to an IQ two standard deviations or more (SD = 15) from the mean IQ of 100 (an IQ of 70 or below). In practical terms, this means a child will have significant problems in reading, writing, arithmetic, memory, attention, and problem solving (although individual children may have strengths in particular areas) (Luckasson et al., 2002). A significant limitation in adaptive behavior refers to how well people cope with common life demands and problems and how well they meet the standards of personal independence expected of someone about their age, community setting, sociocultural background. Adaptive behaviors include taking care of one self, handling money, living in the community, and displaying appropriate behaviors (APA, 2000; Luckasson et al., 2002).

Children with ID comprise a broad spectrum from relatively mild ID (IQ closer to 70) to those with more severe ID (those with IQ below 40). In addition, there a variety of causes of intellectual disabilities ranging from biological/genetic causes (e.g., Down syndrome, Fragile X syndrome), environmental causes (e.g., fetal alcohol syndrome), and educational/social causes (severely limited stimulation). As a result it is difficult to generalize functional abilities (including motor abilities and delays) across the generic classification of ID.

With regards to motor development, limited research shows children with mild ID tend to be one to three years delayed in motor development while children with more severe intellectual disabilities tend to have delays of four years or more (DiRocco, Clark, & Phillips, 1987; Rarick, 1980). These delays are both quantitative (Zhang, 2005; Yun & Ulrich, 1997) and qualitative (DiRocco et al., 1987). These motor delays tend to widen as children with ID grow older and motor performance relies on greater speed and movement control as well as the use of strategies (Sherrill, 2004; Wall, 2004). For example, Zhang (2005) found children ages 12-15 with mild intellectual disabilities scored between 6-10 years delayed compared to peers without ID on the Bruininks-Oseretsky Test of Motor Proficiency.

Children with ID, because of particular biological/genetic causes, often have physical anomalies that lead to specific and more pronounced motor delays and deficits. This is perhaps most notable in children with Down syndrome, a genetic disorder that causes pervasive developmental delays (Pueschel, 2000). Among many other issues, children with Down syndrome have hypotonia ((low muscle tone), increased flexibility in joints, decreased muscle strength, and medical problems such as heart and respiratory problems which all affect and limit motor development (Block, 1991; Pueschel, 2000; Winders, 1997).

Teaching and Coaching Children with Intellectual Disability

The combination of intellectual and adaptive behavior deficits coupled with motor delays in children with intellectual disabilities requires unique teaching methods. In most cases these unique teaching methods focus on presenting information so that individuals with ID will understand what to do and how to do it as well as staying focused on the task at hand. (Drane & Block, 2006; Krebs, 2005). *Communication* is the perhaps the most important teaching strategy. Children with ID may not understand verbal directions imitate demonstrations as well as their peers. This requires the teacher or coach to simplify verbal directions and highlight key components of a demonstration. For example, a coach may point to the inside of his foot, touch the child's inside foot, and then have the child touch a ball to the inside of his foot in order to make sure the child understand where to contact the ball when passing a soccer ball. When verbal and visual cues do not work, the coach or teacher may need to provide physical assistance.

"Attention" is another key teaching strategy when working with children with ID. Children with ID often do not have the attention span of their peers without ID, and as a result they have a difficult time staying focused when practicing a skill or staying focused on a key aspect of a skill (Drane & Block, 2006; Krebs, 2005). For example, a teacher may ask children to pick up a ball and practice their overhand throw against the wall. The teacher specifically tells children to focus on stepping with the opposite foot. The child with ID may throw a few balls remembering to step with the opposite foot, but quickly the student becomes distracted losing focus first on stepping with the opposite foot and eventually practicing the throw at all. To combat this problem, teachers and coaches need to organize the practice setting to help the child with ID stay focused. This includes making practice very concrete such as placing 20 balls in front of the child telling him to throw each ball one at a time until all the balls are gone. The teacher may place foot print or other visual cues on the floor to remind the child to focus on a particular component. The teacher may need to go to the child more often than to peers without ID to remind to keep him focused and provide extra instruction and reinforcement.

Finally, a peer can assigned to the child during a particular activity to provide extra cues.

Finally, teachers and coaches should plan on dealing with *behavior problems* often displayed by children with ID. Behavior problems tend to be fairly mild (e.g., refusing to participate, walking away, playing with equipment inappropriately) revolving around frustration with lack of success, confusion with what to do, boredom, and wanting to exert some control. Strategies to combat behavior problems focus on understanding the root cause or the function of the problem (Block, 2007). For example, a child with an ID refuses to take his turn to hit a pitched baseball. This child may know from previous experiences that he cannot hit a pitched ball, and his refusal to participate is an indication of lack of confidence based on previous experience. In this situation the teacher or coach can offer a lighter, larger bat or allow the child to hit a ball off a tee. Similarly, a child with an ID tries to hit a peer after the teacher gives complex directions on how to rotate to various stations in the gym. The child is telling the teacher he does not know what to do, and this confusion lead to anxiety and acting out. Knowing ahead of time the child with ID may not understand directions; after directing the group the teacher immediately goes to this child and repeats the directions in a simpler form. The teacher may even walk the child over to the first station to help him get started.

CHILDREN WITH LEARNING DISABILITIES

Specific learning disability (SLD) defines a group of disabilities that affect a child's ability to learn which in turn affects a child's academic performance. Deficits are neurologically based, and damage to specific parts of the brain will determine specific types of learning disabilities (Lavay, 2005; Shapiro, 2001). For example, one child may have a learning disability in reading while another child may have a learning disability in math (see Table 1 for a list of specific types of learning disabilities). Children with SLD do not have any intellectual disabilities and in some cases may even be quite gifted and do extraordinary things. Famous people with learning disabilities include Walt Disney, Albert Einstein, and General George Patton (LD Online, 2008). It is important to note that to have the label of learning disability a child cannot have other disabilities that might affect learning such as in intellectual disability, autism, deafness, blindness, and behavioral disorders. Also, a learning disability cannot occur suddenly by a lack of educational opportunities, attendance problems, or frequent changes of schools. Reported incidence of SLD ranges from as low as 5% of the school age population to as high as 15%. The discrepancy may be due to children who qualify for special education services (5%) compared to children who may have some type of a learning disability but who many not qualify for special education. Reading disabilities are the most common type of SLD comprising almost 80% of all learning disabilities (LD Online, 2008; Shapiro, 2001).

Table 1. Specific Types of Learning Disabilities*

Dyslexia – the most common type of learning disability, dyslexia refers to a language-based disability in which the child has trouble understanding written words including basic reading (decoding letters and words), reading comprehension (understanding what to read), spelling, and writing. Dyslexia is related to problems with visual perception, the ability to notice important visual details.

Dyscalculia – a mathematical disability in which a person has a difficult time with arithmetic problems and grasping math concepts. Specific mathematic problems can include math reasoning, memory of math facts, concepts of time and money, and musical concepts.

Dysgraphia – Also known as graphomotor disorder, dysgraphia is a writing disability where children finds it difficult to form letters and write within a defined space as well as the speed and precision in writing. Dyscalculia is often associated with dyslexia.

Dyspraxia (**apraxia**) – dyspraxia is a motor planning disability where the child had difficulty coordinating movements. These children appear awkward in their movements and may also have balance problems. Another term for dyspraxia is developmental coordination disorder (DCD).

Auditory Discrimination – auditory discrimination is an auditory disability in which a person has difficulty understanding language despite normal hearing. Auditory discrimination problems make it difficult for children to perceive differences between speech sounds then sequence sounds into meaningful words. Auditory processing also makes it difficult to understand the phonetics sounds of letters which is critical for learning to read.

From LD Online. *Common Learning Disabilities*. Retrieved November 10, 2008, from http://www.ldonline.org/ldbasics/whatisld.

About 25 to 50% of children with SLD have other disabilities or problems. The most common related disability is attention deficit/hyperactive disorder (ADHD) (see discussion later in this chapter). Some children with SLD also have behavior or emotional problems. Behavior problems may be due to neurological impairments that may lead to depression or anxiety disorders. On the other hand, many children with SLD who display behavior problems may be reacting negatively to their academic difficulties (Shapiro, 2001). Imagine a 4th grade child with dyslexia who still struggles with reading. This child sees his peers moving to more advanced books while he still is barely able to read 1st grade material. It is not surprising that this child might have issues with self-esteem which in turn might lead to anxiety, depression, and withdrawal when faced with academic work. Or perhaps this child may get frustrated and angry with his struggles with reading which leads to acting out and conduct behaviors. In either case, behavior problems are directly related to the child's learning disability and how it affects academic performance. This is why it is so important to identify learning disabilities as soon as possible so a child does not struggle academically and can get some remedial help.

Many children with learning disabilities do not have any gross motor problems and are actually quite athletic. Some famous athletes who had learning disabilities include Olympic gold medalist Bruce Jenner, basketball star Magic Johnson, football start Dexter Manley, and baseball star Pete Rose (Angle, 2007). However, some children with learning disabilities also have motor problems. Not surprisingly, motor problems are most notable in children with motor and sensory related learning problems such as dyspraxia and visual processing problems (Shapiro, 2001). For example, Miyahara (1994) found 25% of children with SLD scored poorly in a general motor ability test, and an additional 7% demonstrated significant balance problems. Similarly, Lazarus (1994) found children with SLD had greater levels of overflow (an inability to keep one arm or leg still while moving the other arm or leg) compared to same-age peers without SLD. Finally, Sherrill and Pyfer (1985) found 13 percent of children with LD scored 2-3 years below age level on perceptual motor tests. Again, these motor difficulties seem to be related to motor planning (dyspraxia) (e.g., Lazarus and Miyahara) and visual perception (Sherrill & Pyfer, 1985).

Teaching and Coaching Strategies for Children with Specific Learning Disabilities

Special teaching and coaching strategies for children with learning disabilities are similar to those for children with ADHD. Strategies are designed to help these students stay focused on and understand the activity.

Some additional strategies are needed to compensate for perceptual and movement problems. The following suggestions are adapted from Lavay (2005), Sherrill (2004), Drane and Block (2006):

1. Use a highly structured, consistent approach to teaching (i.e., establish a routine, have set places for children to sit, use a direct rather than exploratory approach when possible).
2. Include activities during warm-ups and cool downs that emphasize moving slowly to help control to decrease hyperactivity and impulsivity.
3. When necessary, teach in a quiet, less stimulating environment to decrease distractibility.
4. Assign a peer to provide extra instruction and assistance to a child who is having trouble moving correctly.
5. Encourage children to plan out loud and repeat directions to enhance motor planning. This is especially important for disorganized, distractible children.
6. Provide appropriate learning strategies to help disorganized learners focus on skill (tell class objective of lesson, ID critical elements of skill, use extra cues such as footprints on floor; teach students how to practice and use feedback).
7. Use a multisensory approach when giving instruction to students with perceptual problems. For example, give a direction verbally, demonstrate the skill, have the students mirror your demonstration, and even provide physical guidance as needed.
8. Eliminate embarrassing teaching practices that force comparison among students. For example, do not have a child with an SLD who is clumsy demonstrate in front of the class unless you know the child will be successful.
9. Use cooperative teaching styles to increase student's social interaction and self-concept.
10. Review previously acquired skills to make sure child has achieved mastery. Occasionally review previously mastered skills when introducing new skills to further enhance long-term retention.

Include perceptual and motor activities in the curriculum such as balance, body awareness, eye-hand coordination, and tactile/visual/auditory stimulation. P-M activities can easily be added as a station. For example, several soccer stations can be set up in the gym, and an additional station can be set up where children have to run through a rope ladder followed by leaping from one poly spot to another.

Children with Attention Deficit Hyperactivity Disorder (ADHD)

Attention Deficit/Hyperactivity Disorder (ADHD) is a disorder that makes it significantly difficult for children to pay attention, focus on a task, and sit still. There are two main types of ADHD. In the hyperactive-impulsive type children appear extremely energized and overactive (hyperactive) and unable to anticipate consequences of their behaviors (impulsivity). In the inattentive type children may be inattentive, have difficulty focusing, and may seem to be daydreaming or lack motivation. There is a third type (*combined*) in which both types of behaviors are present (APA, 2000; Glanzman & Blum, 2007). Table 2 presents the diagnostics criteria for ADHD from the American Psychiatric Association (APA, 2000).

ADHD affects approximately 1/20 children. It is 3 times more common in boys than girls, and usually appears when children start school and are asked to sit and pay attention for extending periods of time (NICHCY, 2001; Glanzman & Blum, 2007). ADHD characteristics can range from mild to severe with far more children being diagnosed with mild ADHD. An interesting note about children with mild ADHD is they seem to be able to focus and attend when they are participating in a highly motivating activity such as playing a video game or when they are given a novel activity (Glanzman & Blum, 2007).

As noted earlier, primary characteristics associated with ADHD revolve around problems with attention, impulsivity, and hyperactivity. However, children with ADHD often have problems that are directly related to these primary problems. In turn, these associated problems tend to be interrelated. For example, many children with ADHD have problems developing friendships and interacting appropriately with peers. Problems with peers are most likely related to the child's difficulty paying attention (e.g., not attending to peers) and hyperactivity (difficulty staying still or in one place). In addition, attention problems make it difficult for a child to pick up on peer's facial expressions, body language, and the flow of a conversation. As a result peers perceive the child with ADHD as uninterested in them and a nuisance, and as a result the child with ADHD may be isolated and even ostracized by peers. A child with ADHD who is isolated and not included may develop a lower self-esteem and becomes more susceptible to antisocial conduct disorders such as acting out, fighting, running away, and drug use. Some suggest as many as 30-50% of children with ADHD have these antisocial behaviors (Moffitt, 1990; Werry, Elkind & Reeves, 1987; Woolrich, 1994).

Somewhat surprisingly, motor delays are another characteristic often associated with ADHD. While many children with ADHD do quite well in physical education and sport, many others show signs of gross motor delays (Harvey & Reid, 2003). For example, Harvey and Reid (1997) found children with ADHD scored lower on the Test of Gross Motor Development (TGMD) (a test that measures basic fundamental motor skills such as throwing and catching and running and jumping) when compared to peers without ADHD. Kadesjo and Gillberg (1998) and Peik, Pitcher, and Hay (1999) found 50% of children with ADHD they studied had developmental coordination disorder (DCD), a significant impairment in general motor coordination and control. Yan and Thomas (2002), found children with ADHD took more time and were less accurate and more variable completing a rapid arm movement task compared to children without ADHD. Finally, Beyer (1999) found boys with ADHD 7 to 12 years of age performed significantly poorer in fine motor and motor coordination timed tests compared to children with learning disabilities. Interestingly, there were no differences in balance and upper limb coordination tests. It is possible that children with ADHD do poorly in timed and accuracy tests (e.g., Beyer, 1999, and Yan & Thomas, 2002) because of difficulties with impulsivity (moving without thinking) and attention to exact movement requirements of the task. Similarly, tests that measure developmental coordination (Kadesjo & Gillberg, 1998; and Piek, et al., 1999) often require attending to a task and moving carefully, something that may be difficult for children with ADHD. It is less clear why some children with ADHD would have problems with fundamental motor patterns at seen in Harvey and Reid's study (2003).

Teaching and Coaching Strategies for Children with ADHD

Sherrill (2004) presented several suggestions for teaching children with ADHD. Since most of the problems associated with ADHD are behavioral rather than physical, the suggestions focus on managing the environment to help the child with ADHD focus.

Establish a Highly Structured Program

To prevent distractibility and to compensate for a short attention span, instructors should establish a routine and follow it as closely as possible. This routine should include a consistent entry routine (how children should enter the gym and where they should go and sit), a relatively set order of activities, a consistent place to received instructions, and even personal space markers such as poly spots and carpet squares (perhaps just for the child with ADHD). Once a routine is established it is important to explain rules and consequences and remind the child often of these rules and consequences. In some cases a special behavior management plan might need to be established just for the child with disabilities. Whether class-wide rules or a specific behavior plan, it is important for the instructor to follow the plan as designed. While the child may not enjoy having to sit out or have a piece of equipment taken away for a few minutes, he will appreciate the consistency. It also is important to provide positive reinforcement when the child is doing what he is supposed to be doing.

Reduce Wait Time and Have Clear Start/Stop Signals

Children with ADHD cannot sit and focus for long periods of time. A simple way to help them focus on directions in is to reduce how long a child sits and listens to directions, For example, rather than explaining in detail what to do at five different stations, provide a quick demonstration at each station and then post more detailed directions and different challenges at each station. Then children can be assigned to stations and start the activity. Peers can or the instructor can help those students who do not understand what to do. Similarly, keep transition times to a minimum, and have clear stop commands. For example, a nice auditory cue is music playing while children work at a station. When the music is turned off, that is a cue to stop, sit and listen for instructions. Peers can add an extra verbal reminder to the child with ADHD to help him know to stop. Finally, the instructor can position him/herself close to the child and provide a pre-cue to let the child know that it will be time to stop in 30 seconds.

Reduce Environmental Space

Children with ADHD often cannot handle large open spaces or spaces without any clear boundaries. Therefore, it is important to delimit large spaces by adding partitions and floor markers. Special emphasis should be given to boundaries and how to make these boundaries visually clear to the child. Cones, tape markings, and ropes are good boundary markers, while gym mats can turn into an attractive nuisance (i.e., the child may find the mats attractive to jump on).

Eliminate Irrelevant Auditory and Visual Stimuli

A child with ADHD will be easily distracted by extraneous things in the gym, so it is important to maintain neat, uncluttered, well-ordered gym. As noted above, create partitions to keep children from looking at other stations or equipment, and try to avoid setting up equipment until needed. When giving instructions try and stand so that children see only you and not other distractors in environment. For example, if you are outside giving instructions, position yourself so the children have their back to other children playing on the playground.

Enhance Stimulus Value of Instructional Materials

To help children with ADHD focus on the targeted task, use brightly colored objects and markers such as balls and targets. Color coding activities can help as well such as throwing red balls to a red target. When possible, use auditory equipment (balls with bells) to provide further motivation to the child. Finally use mirrors so that children can look at themselves when performing an activity. In all of these cases enhanced stimulation will help the child focus.

CHILDREN WITH AUTISM

Autism is part of the larger cluster of disabilities known as pervasive developmental disorder (PDD). PDDs comprise a spectrum of similar disorders that affect communication, behaviors, and social skills. The term spectrum connotes a range in the severity of the characteristics from relatively mild (children with Asperger syndrome) to severe (children with Rett disorder). There is a spectrum within the classification of autism with some children having relatively mild communication, behavioral, and social deficits while others may display more severe deficits. Whether mild or severe, the deficits and unique behaviors that characterize autism are not typical for the child's developmental age. Table 3 presents the diagnostics criteria for autistic disorder from the American Psychiatric Association (APA, 2000).

Table 3. Diagnostic Criteria for Autistic Disorder*

A. A total of six (or more) items from (1), (2), and (3), with at least two from (1), and on each from (2) and (3):

1) Qualitative impairment in social interaction, as manifested by at least two of the following:

   a. Marked impairment in the use of multiple nonverbal behaviors such as eye-to-eye gaze, facial expression, body postures, and gestures to regulate social interactions.

   b. Failure to develop peer relationships appropriate to developmental level.

   c. A lack of spontaneous seeking to share enjoyment, interests, or achievements with other people (e.g., by a lack of showing, bringing, or pointing out objects of interest).

   d. ack of social or emotional reciprocity.

2) Qualitative impairments in communication as manifested by at least one of the following:

   a. Delay in, or total lack of, the developmental of spoken language (not accompanied by an attempt to compensate through alternative modes of communication such as gestures or mime).

   b. In individuals with adequate speech, marked impairment in the ability to initiate or sustain a conversation with others.

   c. Stereotyped and repetitive use of language or idiosyncratic language.

   d. Lack of varied, spontaneous make-believe play or social imitative play appropriate to developmental level.

3) Restricted repetitive and stereotyped patterns of behavior, interests, and activities as manifested by at least one of the following:

   a. Encompassing preoccupation with one or more stereotyped and restricted patterns of interest that is abnormal either in intensity or focus.

   b. Apparently inflexible adherence to specific, nonfunctional routines or rituals.

   c. Stereotyped and repetitive motor mannerisms (e.g., hand or finger flapping or twisting, or complex whole-body movements).

   d. Persistent preoccupation with parts of objects.

B. Delays or abnormal functioning in at least one of the following areas, with onset prior to age 3 years: (1) social interactions, (2) language as used in social communication, or (3) symbolic or imaginative play.

C. The disturbance is not better accounted for by Rett's Disorder or Childhood Disintegrative Disorder.

American Psychological Association (APA) (2000). *Diagnostic and statistical manual of mental disorders* (4th ed, TR). Washington, DC.

Communication deficits are one of the characteristics of autism. In the most severe cases children with autism may have no speech or even an ability to communicate using sign language, but often these children learn to point to things they want, take a parents hand and lead them to an item, or use a picture board and point to pictures showing wanted items. In other cases children with autism learn to speak but at an inappropriate level (e.g., whisper or too loud for the context) or in inappropriate ways (Powers, 1989; Towbin, 2001). For example, some children with autism may repeat certain words that create an interesting sound or interesting feeling in their mouth. In other cases, children echo what was asked. To illustrate, when asked, "How are you, John?" the child repeats the question, "How are you, John?" In addition to expressive language deficits, children with autism also have a difficult time understanding verbal language. In very severe cases, parents reported they thought their child was deaf because their child was completely unresponsive to any speech or sounds. In mild cases, a child with autism may not understand multiple directions when give verbally or may not understand abstract, pretend, or sarcastic speech (Powers, 1989; Towbin, 2001). For example, a physical educator tells the class to pretend the gym floor is water and carpet squares are islands. He then tells the class to jump from one "island" to another without falling into the water. The child with autism may start to cry worried he may actually get wet or even drown.

Social deficits are another characteristic of children with autism and perhaps the one most associated with autism. Children with autism have a very difficult time interacting appropriately including making eye contact with others, playing with others, sharing toys, and seeking to be with others. Children with autism often do not seem interested in being with, interacting with, and enjoying others company (Mundy & Sigman, 1989; Powers, 1989; Towbin, 2001). However, limited social interactions do not mean children with autism do want to interact with parents and peers. Unfortunately, these children often lack communication and behavioral skills necessary to initiate and sustain contact. In addition, it is important to note that children with autism do not always want to be alone and may enjoy cuddling- up with or hugging a parent or sibling.

Unique behaviors are the final major characteristic associated with autism. In many cases unique and odd behaviors is the first thing that differentiates children with autism from their peers. As with other characteristics associated with autism, behaviors can range from mild mannerisms such as rocking or shaking hands to more severe behaviors including self-abuse, tantrums, and aggression. Many feel the more severe behaviors are associated with limited communication skills. In other words, a child becomes frustrated when he cannot tells someone what he wants or does not understand what to do. In addition, children with autism like routines and "sameness," and sudden changes in routines can lead to unwanted behaviors. Another unique behavioral characteristic associated with autism is inappropriate play with toys and objects. For example, a child with autism might repeatedly spin the wheels on a toy car rather than playing with the car like same-age peers. Similarly, a child may line up objects in a certain way but never actually play with the objects. A final behavioral idiosyncrasy associated with autism is sensitivity to sensory stimulations. Some children with autism might be sensitive to touch, others might be sensitive to sounds, and still others may be sensitive to light and visual stimulation. In severe cases children may wear ear phones to block out extraneous sounds in the environment while other children may not like to wear certain clothes or like being touched (Block, Block, & Halliday, 2006; Powers, 1989; Towbin, 2001).

Motor delays are usually considered a common characteristic of autism (Reid & Collier, 2002), but some feel that children with autism do not have any true motor delays or deficits and can demonstrate some fairly advanced, unique motor skills (e.g., Sigman & Capps, 1997). For example, it is not uncommon for parents to comment anecdotally that their child displays excellent balance and climbing skills (can easily traverse even advanced playground structures), can run, gallop, even skip when in an open field, and can manipulate small and complex objects easily. Unfortunately, these same well coordinated and athletic looking children do not do well when given formal motor tests. For example, Slavoff (1997) found all of the 13 pre-K through 3rd grade children she tested using the gross-motor section of the Peabody Developmental Motor Scales (PDMS) scored significantly below their peers. The gross motor section of the PDMS measures motor development using quantitative measures of balance (e.g., standing on one foot, walking a balance beam), locomotion (run, jump, gallop), and object manipulation (catching a tossed ball). Similarly, Berkeley, Zittel, Pitney, and Nichols (2001) found seventy-five percent of their sample of children with high functioning autism ages 6-8 scored at a level that that was significantly delayed compared to peers on the Test of Gross Motor Development (TGMD). The TGMD tests qualitative aspects of locomotor (e.g., run, gallop) and object control (e.g., throw, catch) skills. Finally, Manjiviona and Prior (1995) found that two-thirds of their sample of high functioning children with autism ages 7-17 performed at a delayed level on the Test of Motor Impairment-Henderson Revision (TOMI). The TOMI evaluates motor abilities in children such manual dexterity (sorting objects), ball skills (catching a ball), and balance (walking on a beam, standing on one foot).

While all three studies clearly showed children with autism having significant motor delays, it still is unclear whether these delays are purely motor in nature or due to lack of motivation, attention, and understanding the task. For example, all three tests used in the study measures jumping either qualitatively (TGMD) or quantitatively (PDMS, TOMI). To score well in a jumping test one needs to forcefully swing arms back and then forward and forcefully bend then extend legs. While most children with autism can jump very easily, children with autism tend to not move forcefully (at least not on command). Whether due to lack of motivation or not understanding exactly what to do, the result is children with autism would not score well on jumping items. Similarly, some items on the TOMI are timed (e.g., sort objects or stringing bead as quickly as possible) and some items on the TGMD and PDMS (e.g., running) require a child to move quickly. Again, whether a lack of interest, short attention span, or some other reason, most children with autism do not do well when asked to move quickly, and as a result may not score well on these types of items.

Teaching and Coaching Strategies for Children with Autism

Children with autism require unique teaching strategies that help take advantage of their strengths while accommodating their unique behaviors and learning deficits. There are many strategies that can be employed to help children with autism be more successful in physical education.

Setting up the Environment

The first general strategy focuses on setting up the environment that takes advantage of the child's visual strengths (many children with autism respond much better to visual rather than verbal cues). Setting up a visual environment also prevents behavior outbursts which often occur when a child is confused with the environment or what to do. Specific strategies for setting up the environment include organizing the physical layout so that it clearly explains to the child where to go and what to do (e.g., poly spots to sit on when the child enters the gym, pictures on stations to show the child what to do, and equipment set up in such a way that the child clearly understand what to do with the equipment. Establishing a clear routine with a visual schedule also is helpful for children with autism. The visual schedule explains via pictures everything the child will do in physical education (e.g., stretches, run laps, ride stationary bike, throw to target, kick to target, stretch, and leave the gym). Related to the visual schedule is establishing a routine and having a clear ending to the class. Children with autism often have difficulties with transition from one place to another and from one activity to another. A routine can be as simple as always sitting down on a poly spot when entering the gym followed by a review of the visual schedule followed by stretching as a group. It also is important to have clear, consistent closure to session to help the child understand physical education is over and it is time to move to another activity (Blubaugh & Kohlmann, 2006; Groft-Jones & Block, 2006).

Communication

How to present information is critical for children with autism. As noted, above many children with autism respond better to visual cues rather than verbal cues. However, children with autism can respond to verbal cues under certain conditions (Sigman & Capps, 1997). **First, get the child's attention and try and get eye-contact with the child. Any child who is not focused on the instructor's verbal cues will do poorly, so it is imperative to get the child's attention.** Asking the child to follow simple directions you know the child can do such as touching body parts often breaks a child away from a daydreaming state to a state of focus. Once the child is attending to the instructor, use very **simple verbal directions. For example, rather than saying "watch me as I throw the ball, and pay particular attention to how I step with my opposite foot,"** say "watch me" (then demonstrate the throwing exaggerating the stepping motion), followed by "you do it." Similarly, avoid verbal jargon that might confuse the child with autism. For example, saying "gallop like a horse" might confuse a child who does not know how a horse gallops or who does not understand how he (the child with two legs) can gallop like a horse with four legs. Finally, as noted above use alternative forms of communication including pictures, gestures, signs language, and environmental cues. For example, an instructor might demonstrate a proper kick in soccer, and he also shows a child a picture of a player kicking a soccer ball. Then the instructor puts a red footprint next the ball to show the child where to step (environmental cue). He **also places a red piece of tape on the child's left foot. Now the child is told to** step on the red spot with the red show and kick the ball. Simplifying cues and instruction often allows children with autism to respond to verbal cues, but pairing verbal cues with visual cues is probably the best solution (Groft-Jones & Block, 2006).

Prevent Challenging Behaviors

Communication and social deficits often result in children with autism getting confused with their environment and what to do. This confusing can lead to behavioral outbursts directed at teachers, peers or even back towards the child him/herself (known as self-abusive behaviors). Teachers and coaches should be aware of challenging behaviors and try to avoid situations that lead to these behaviors. Many of the suggestions above (e.g., visual schedules, routines, keeping communication simple) are a good start to preventing behavior problems. It also is important to let the child know that he/she is doing the activity or skill correctly. That is why it is important to provide a lot of positive reinforcement to the child when he/she does do the activity correctly (or even attempts to activity). For example, if you ask a child run and he attempts to run by doing a fast walk, the instructor would still reinforce the child (**"good running Johnny, let's try again lifting our feet** higher off the ground. Watch me run …. Now you do it."). **Positive reinforcement** includes finding a powerful reinforce the child wants to earn by following directions. This reinforce might start out with food and gradually fade to bouncing on a therapy ball or riding a scooter. Children with autism also need to be taught and then reinforced on appropriate behaviors and appropriate play and use of equipment. For example, a child might turn a scooter board over and just play with the wheels. The instructor would go to the student, turn the scooter back over, and show him how to ride the scooter. When the child does ride the scooter the teacher would provide praise and perhaps a treat for playing appropriately, reinforcing appropriate behaviors. Despite best efforts to prevent behavioral outburst, children with autism may get frustrated with an activity or may get over stimulated with sensory input (environment is too loud or the lights are too bright for the child). Dealing with challenging behaviors when they do occur should first eliminate the cause of the problem (e.g., turn down the music **or place earphones on the child' ears** to muffle the sound), remove the child from the activity or setting if possible, and having a calming activity for the child such as lying on a matt or rolling on a therapy ball. Often gently removing the child from the environment and allowing the child to do a calming activity will quickly end the behavior problem (MacDonald, Jones, and Istone, 2006).

CHILDREN WITH VISUAL IMPAIRMENTS

The term visual impairment is a global term describing someone who has a significant visual loss that cannot be adequately corrected by glasses (Holbrook, 2006). Vision and visual impairment are measured two ways: visual acuity and field of vision. V*isual acuity* measures how clearly one can see from a standard distance. Visual acuity is measured using the Snellen chart which contains letters of the alphabet arranged by line with each line decreasing in size. For younger children the Lighthouse Flash Card Test is used with pictures or shapes substituting for letters). To test vision the subject stands 20' (6.1 meters) away from the chart. The bottom line represents 20/20 vision and the single letter on the top represents 20/200 vision. A person with normal visual acuity (20/20 vision) can read all the lines on the chart including the bottom line (Miller & Menacker, 2007). Legal blindness is defined as 20/200 vision even with corrective glasses, so a person who is legally blind would be able to read only the top letter from 20'. Put another way, a person with 20/200 vision sees at 20' what a person with normal vision sees at 200' (Holbrook, 2006; Miller & Menacker, 2007). Those with more severe visual impairments would not be able to even read the top letter.

Field of vision measures the total area that can be seen without moving the eyes or head. To test visual field the subject sits still focusing on forward on a spot on the wall. Objects are then slowly moved from behind the subject into the subject's visual field. The subject tells the examiner the object can be seen, and the examiner records the visual field. Young children can sit in a parent's lap and do this test with a favorite object or toy slowly brought into the child's visual field. A normal visual field is 160-170 degrees, and a visual impairment is considered a visual field of 20 degrees or less in the better eye. Some people have both visual acuity and visual field losses, while others just have one or the other (Holbrook, 2006; Miller & Menacker, 2007). Table 4 provides a definition of various levels of visual impairment based on visual acuity.

Visual impairment describes a functional loss of vision. Various eye disorders can result to a visual impairment. Some of the more common types of eye disorders include can include retinal degeneration, albinism, cataracts, glaucoma, muscular problems that result in visual disturbances (e.g., strabismus, nystagmus), corneal disorders, diabetic retinopathy, congenital disorders (cortical blindness), and infection. These disorders can cause partial or complete visual loss (NICHCY, 2004) (see Holbrook, 2006, for more detailed descriptions).

Table 4. Classification of Visual Impairment Based on Visual Acuity*

Acuity	Visual Impairment	Functional Description
20/70	Partial sighted	Some type of visual problem has resulted in a need for special education
20/70-20/200	Low vision	Visual impairment, not necessarily limited to distance vision. Low vision applies to all individuals with sight who are unable to read the newspaper at a normal viewing distance, even with the aid of eyeglasses or contact lenses. They use a combination of vision and other senses to learn, although they may require adaptations in lighting or the size of print, and, sometimes, Braille; also includes a visual field of 20 degrees or less.
20/200	Legally blind	Can see from 20' what a sighted person can see from 200'. Will require Braille or books on tape.
5/200-10/200	Motion perception	Sees 5-10' what a sighted person can see at 200'. Can detect movement from 3-5' away but cannot say what is moving.
3/200	Light perception	Can detect a strong light at a distance of 3' but unable to detect movement at 3' from eye.
0	Total blindness	Inability to recognize a strong light straight into eye.

* Modified from Lieberman, L.J. (2005). Visual impairments. In J.P. Winnick (ed.). *Adapted physical education and sport* (4th ed.). (pp. 205-219). Champaign, IL: Human Kinetics., and National Dissemination Center for Children with Disabilities (NICHCY) (2004). *Visual Impairments – Fact Sheet 13*. Retrieved November 22, 2008m from http://old.nichcy.org/pubs/factshe/fs13txt.htm.

Most children with a visual impairment do not have intellectual or physical disabilities (although some can have multiple disabilities). However, visual loss can have a significant effect on overall development. The effect of visual loss on a child's development depends on many factors including the type of disorder and severity of loss, age at which the condition appears, and overall functioning level of the child (NICHCY, 2004). Of particular importance for normal development is whether a child is born with a visual impairment (congenital) or acquires a visual loss later in childhood (acquired) (Holbrook, 2006; NICHCY, 2004). Social development is a particularly delayed in children born with visual impairments. Early social development is dependent on visual observation including preverbal communication (e.g., gesturing, understanding non-verbal cues) and social reciprocity (taking turns and social imitation). These delays are most notable in children with visual impairments of 20/500 or greater. However, these delays are usually overcome as the child develops (Miller & Menacker, 2007).

Motor Delays

Motor delays are often found in children with visual impairments. Motor delays are not neurologically or motor related but rather due to lack of the ability to observe others. A child who is born with a visual impairment or acquires a visual impairment very early in childhood has little reason to explore interesting objects in the environment. This results in missed opportunities and experiences that effect motor development and learning. Lack of exploration may continue until learning becomes motivated or until intervention begins (Fraiberg, 1977). In addition, a child may actually fear movement, and parents often are concerned their child may get injured which further limits motor exploration and normal rough and tumble play (Lieberman, 2005; Miller & Menacker, 2007). Early locomotor patterns are most affected by visual loss including crawling, creeping, cruising, and walking with delays of 4-6 months, while stationary patterns such as sitting show only a 1-2 month delay (Fraiberg, 1977; Hatton, Bailey, & Burchinal, 1997). Children with visual impairments eventually catch up and develop these and other locomotor skills. However, it is common for children with visual impairments to have a unique walking pattern noted by a slow, shuffling gait with a wide base of support. Again, this is due to not being able to see where one is going rather than any neurological delays (Lieberman, 2005).

Other motor problems associated with children with visual impairments include postural deviations and hypotonia. Hypotonia is low muscle tone which is a direct byproduct of limited movement. Postural problems are related to hypotonia and an inability to observe normal postures. Both of these conditions usually correct themselves as a child begins early intervention and becomes more active. However, children with visual impairments tend have muscle tone and overall physical fitness delays well into childhood and adolescence (Lieberman & McHugh, 2001); Winnick & Short, 1986). Balance also may be a problem in children with visual impairments, and again these delays are related to lack of movement experiences and practice. In addition, balance is aided by focusing on a reference point which is obviously not available to children with visual impairments (Lieberman, 2005). Finally, children with congenital visual impairments tend to take longer to learn object control skills such as throwing and kicking, and often never develop a smooth, integrated pattern when performing these skills. For example, it is more difficult to learn all the components of an overhand throw when a child has never seen what a skillful throw looks or receives visual feedback. On the other hand, children who have already acquired object control skills before losing their vision should not have any of these problems with object control skills.

Teaching and Coaching Strategies for Children with Visual Impairments

Teaching strategies for children with visual impairments focus on how to present information using other means other than vision (Drane & Block, 2006; Lieberman, 2005). Demonstration will only be useful for children with visual impairments of 20/200 or better, and you will want to place the child as close to you as possible for the demonstration. Verbal explanations will be more important for children with visual impairments, and these verbal cues need to be very specific. Providing a verbal cue for throwing such as "put your arm over here" is too general for a child with a visual impairment. A more appropriate cue would be "when throwing bring your arm back so that your hand is behind your ear and your elbow is pointing towards the target." Physical guidance also will be an important teaching tool with the teacher or coach manipulating the child through the correct pattern. Pairing physical guidance with verbal cue words is a good strategy with gradual fading of physical guidance. For example, putting a child into side orientation to the target for the throw can be paired with the cue words "side orientation." After placing the child into side orientation for several trials, the teacher can fad this physical guidance and verbally cue the child with "side orientation." A final tool for communicating how to move to a child with a visual impairment is *tactile modeling* (Lieberman, 2005). Tactile modeling is when you (the teacher) do the movement with the child holding on to you to feel how you move. As you move your arm for the throw, the child places one hand on your elbow and one on your wrist to get a feel for how the movement is performed. Tactile modeling tends to be better for smaller motor skills or components of larger movement skills.

It also is important to enhance targets and boundaries with brighter colors, tactile cues, and sound devices (Lieberman 2005). Children with low vision will appreciate bright contrasts such as yellow tape over a blue floor as well as bright orange cones contrasting a white wall. Placing tape over a rope on the floor provides a raised, tactile surface that makes it easier for a child with a visual impairment to locate a space and to know when he/she is crossing a boundary. Finally, sound devices can be used to help a child with a visual impairment locate targets and equipment. This can be as easy as placing a bell into a ball or putting a portable radio under a target. Peers also can clap to help a child locate a target. Equipment with electronic beepers such as beepers in balls and cones can be purchased.

The type of activity is also important to consider when working with children with visual impairments. *Closed motor skills* are consistent and predictable with stationary target and generally set movements. Throwing to a set target, kicking to a set target, bowling, hitting a golf ball, and archery are good examples of closed skills. *Open motor skills* are those that have variables that change often and thus are unpredictable. Hitting a tennis ball or playing a game of volleyball, soccer or basketball, are examples of open motor skills. Clearly closed motor skills will be easier to teach and will allow more success and independence in children with visual impairments compared to open motor skills (Lieberman, 2005). However, open motor skills and activities can be adjusted to make them closed for the child with a visual impairment. For example, in a volleyball game a peer can catch the ball for a child with a visual impairment, hand it the child, and then let the child do his/her standard serve to a teammate. Similarly, a child can receive a free pass in basketball, and the pass has to be a bounce pass from 10' away followed by the child allowed free pass to teammate who claps to cue the child where to pass.

Finally, safety should be a concern when planning the physical education and sport environment for children with visual impairments. The teacher or coach needs to think from the perspective of the child to analyze the environment for safety concerns. For example, volleyball standards or gym mats stored in the corner of the gym might be a hazard for a child with a visual impairment. Similarly, setting up equipment or stations before children enter the gym can cause an injury. Some equipment cannot be moved, and the best resolution is walking the child through the gym or play environment pointing out permanent objects. On days when equipment is set up ahead of time, make sure the entry way is clear for the child. In addition, explain to the child where equipment is placed around the gym. A clock analogy is often easy for a child with a visual impairment to understand. For example, with the child facing a particular direction the teacher can say "station 1 with cones for dribbling is at 9 o'clock, station 2 has cones and balls on the floor where you will pass with a partner is at 11 o'clock, the shooting station with various size targets on the wall and balls on the floor is at 1 o'clock, and throw-ins with a partner will be a station 4, and I have cones and balls on the floor ready at that station." Peers can provide these extra cues and can be used to guide the child into the gym as well as from activity to activity.

HEARING LOSS TABLE

Table 5. Classification of Hearing Impairment Based on Decibel Level*

Level of Hearing Loss	Decibel Level Loss	Sound Equivalent
Typical or Stand	less than 20dB	
Mild	20-40dB	Cannot hear a whispered conversation in a quiet atmosphere at close range.
Moderate	40-60dB	Atmosphere at close range.
Severe	60-90dB	Cannot hear speech; may only hear loud noises such as a vacuum cleaner or lawn mower at close range.
Profound	90dB+	Cannot hear speech; may only hearextremely loud noises such as a chain saw or the vibrating component of a loud sound.

* Alexander Graham Bell Association for the Deaf and Hard of Hearing (AGBell) (2008). Hearing Loss Chart. Retrieved November 23, 2008, from http://www.agbell.org/DesktopDefault.aspx?p=Hearing_Loss_Chart.

SUMMARY AND CONCLUSIONS

As discussed above, lifespan motor development or performance is an important area of overall human development. Motor skill development and its associated changes in the cognitive and affective domains have a number of theoretical and practical implications. The knowledge of age-related but not age-dependent motor development is a foundation for physical education programs in school, sport programs outside school, and the clinical applications. The studies of "normal" motor development can yield critical information for understanding of "abnormal" motor development and generate important assessment tools or rehabilitation approaches for motor disorders for people of various ages. Age-related changes in physical and motor development are useful for ordinary and special populations in tracking normal development or delay in people of different ages and motor capacities, as well in identifying individuals who have special needs. The course of motor development should be offered to teachers, coaches, recreational leaders, and parents.

REFERENCES

Adolph, K.E., Vereijken, B., & Denny, M.A. (1998). Learning to crawl. *Child Development, 69*(5), 1299-1312.

Alexander Graham Bell Association for the Deaf and Hard of Hearing (AGBell) (2008). *About Hearing Loss.* Retrieved November 23, 2008, from http://www.agbell.org/DesktopDefault.aspx?p=About_Hearing_Loss

American Psychological Association (APA) (2000). *Diagnostic and statistical manual of mental disorders* (4th ed, TR). Washington, DC.

Angle, B. (2007, September). Winning the "game" against learning disabilities. *Coach and Athletic Director.* Retrieved November 10, 2008, from http://findarticles.com/p/articles/mi_m0FIH/is_/ai_n27379279

Berkeley, S.L., Zittel, L.L., Pitney, L.V., & Nichols, S.E. (2001). Locomotor and object control skills of children diagnosed with autism. *Adapted Physical Activity Quarterly, 16*, 403-414.

Beyer, R. (1999). Motor proficiency of boys with attention deficit/hyperactivity disorder and boys with learning disabilities. *Adapted Physical Activity Quarterly, 16*, 403-414.

Block, M.E. (2007). *A teachers' guide to including students with disabilities in general physical education* (3rd ed.). Baltimore: Paul H. Brookes.

Block, M.E. (1991). Motor development in children with Down syndrome: A review of the literature. *Adapted Physical Activity Quarterly, 8*, 179-209.

Block, M.E., Block, V.E., & Halliday, P. (2006). What is autism? *Teaching Elementary Physical Education 17*(6), 7-11.

Blubaugh, N., & Kohlmann, J. (2006). TEACCH model for children with autism. *Teaching Elementary Physical Education 17*(6), 16-19.

References

Bredekamp, S., & Copple, C. (1997). Developmentally appropriate practices in early childhood programs. Washington, D.C.: National Association for the Education of Young Children.

Clark, J.E., & Metcalfe, J.S. (2002). The mountain of motor development: A metaphor. In J.E. Clark and J. Humphrey (Eds.), *Motor development: Research and reviews*. Reston, VA: NASPE Publications.

Clark, J.E., & Whittal, J. (1989). What is motor development: The lessons of history. *Quest, 41*, 183-202.

DiRocco, P. J., Clark, J. E., & Phillips, S.J. (1987). Jumping coordination patterns of mildly mentally retarded children. *Adapted Physical Activity quarterly, 4*, 178-191.

Drane, D., & Block, M.E. (2006). *Accessible golf*. Champaign, IL: Human Kinetics.

Frankenburg, W.K., Dodds, J.B., Fandal, A.W., Kazuk, E., & Cohrs, M. (1992). The Denver II: A major revision and restandardization of the Denver Developmental Screening Test. *Pediatrics, 89*, 91-97.

Fraiberg, S, (1977). *Insights from the blind: Comparative studies of blind and sighted infants*. New York: Perseus Books Group.

Gallahue, D.L., & Ozmun, J.C. (2006). Understanding motor development: Infants, children, adolescents, adults. New York: McGrwa-Hill.

Glanzman, M.M, & Blum, N.J. (2007). Attention Deficits and Hyperactivity. In M.L. Batshaw, L Pellegrino, & N.J. Roizen (Ed.), *When your child has a disability* (6th ed.) (pp. 345-366). Baltimore: Paul H. Brookes.

Groft-Jones, M., & Block, M.E. (2006). Strategies for teaching children with autism in physical education. *Teaching Elementary Physical Education 17*(6), 25-28.

Harvey, W.J., & Reid, G. (2003). Attention deficit/hyperactivity disorder: A review of research on movement skill performance and physical fitness. *Adapted Physical Activity Quarterly, 20*, 1-25.

Harvey, W.J., & Reid, G. (1997). Motor performance of children with attention deficit/hyperactivity disorder: A preliminary investigation. *Adapted Physical Activity Quarterly, 14*, 189-202.

Hatton, D.D., Bailey, D.B., & Burchinal, J.R. (1997). Developmental growth curves of preschool children with visual impairments. *Child Development, 68*, 788—806.

Herer, G.R., Knightly, C.A., & Steinberg, A.G. (2007). Hearing: Sounds and silence. In M.L. Batshaw, L. Pellegrino, & N.J. Roizen (Ed.), *When your child has a disability* (6th ed.) (pp. 157-183). Baltimore: Paul H. Brookes.

Holbrook, M.C. (Ed.). (2006). *Children with visual impairments: A parents' guide (2ⁿᵈ ed.)*. Bethesda, MD: WoodbineKadesjo, B., & Gillberg, C. (1998). Attention deficits and clumsiness in Swedish 7-year-old children. *Developmental Medicine and Child Neurology, 40*, 796-804.

Individuals with Disabilities Education Improvement Act (IDEA) of 2004. 20 U.S.C.

Kadesjo, B., & Gillberg, C. (1998). Attention deficits and clumsiness in Swedish 7-year-old children. *Developmental Medicine and Child Neurology, 40*, 796-804.

Krebs, P.L. (2005). Intellectual Disabilities. In J.P. Winnick (Ed.), Adapted and physical education and sport (4th ed.) (pp. 133-153). Champaign, IL: Human Kinetics.

Lavay, B.W. (2005). Specific learning disabilities. In J.P. Winnick (Ed.), *Adapted physical education and sport* (4th ed.) (pp. 189-204).

LDOnline. *What is a learning disability?* Retrieved November 10, 2008, from http://www.ldonline.org/ldbasics/whatisld.

Lieberman, L.J. (2005). Deafness and Deaf blindness. In J.P. Winnick (ed.). *Adapted physical education and sport* (4th ed.). (pp. 221-234). Champaign, IL: Human Kinetics.

Lieberman, L.J., Volding, L., & Winnick, J.P. (2004). A comparison of the motor development of Deaf children of Deaf parents and hearing parents. American Annals for the Deaf, July.

Lieberman, L.J. (2005). Visual impairments. In J.P. Winnick (ed.). *Adapted physical education and sport* (4th ed.). (pp. 205-219). Champaign, IL: Human Kinetics.

Lieberman, L.J., & McHugh, B.E. (2001). Health-related fitness for children with visual impairments and blindness. *Journal of Visual Impairment and Blindness, 95*(5), 272-286.

Luckasson, R.A., Schalock, R.L., Spitalnik, D.M., Spreat, S., Tassé, M., Snell M.E., Coulter, D.L., Borthwick-Duffy, S.A., Alya Reeve, A., Buntinx, W.H.E., & Ellis, M.C. (2002). *Mental retardation: definition, classification, and systems of supports* (10th ed.). Washington, DC: American Association of Intellectual and Developmental Disabilities.

MacDonald, C., Jones, K., & Istone, M. (2006). Positive behavioral support. *Teaching Elementary Physical Education 17*(6), 20-24.

Malina, R.M., Bouchard, C., & Bar-Or, O. (2004). *Growth, maturation, and physical activity*. (2nd ed). Champaign, IL: Human Kinetics.

Manjiviona, J., & Prior, M. (1995). Comparison of Asperger syndrome and high functioning autistic children on a test of motor impairment. *Journal of Autism and Developmental Disorders, 25,* 23-39.

Miller, M.M., & Menacker, S.J. (2007). Vision: Our window to the World. In M.L. Batshaw, L. Pellegrino, & N.J. Roizen (Ed.). *When your child has a disability* (6th ed.) (pp. 137-155). Baltimore: Paul H. Brookes.

Miyahara, M. (1994). Subtypes of students with learning disabilities based on gross motor function. *Adapted Physical Activity Quarterly, 11,* 368-382.

Moffitt, T.E. (1990). Juvenile delinquency and attention deficit disorder: Boys developmental trajectories from age 3 to age 15. *Child Development, 61,* 893-910.

Mundy, P., & Sigman, M. (1989). Specifying the social impairment in autism. In G. Dawson (Ed.), *Autism – Nature, diagnosis, and treatment* (pp. 34-41). New York: Guilford Press.

National Dissemination Center for Children with Disabilities (NICHCY) (2004). *Deafness and Hearing Loss: Fact sheet No. 3.* Retrieved November 22, 2008 from http://www.nichcy.org/InformationResources/Documents/NICHCY%20PUBS/fs3.pdf

National Information Center for Children and Youth with Disabilities (NICHCY). (2001, December). *NICHCY Fact sheet #19: Attention deficit/hyperactivity disorder.* Washington, DC.

Payne, V.G., & Isaacs, L.D. (2008). *Human motor development: A lifespan approach.* New York: McGraw Hill.

Piek, J.P. (2006). *Infant motor development.* Champaign, IL: Human kinetics.

Piek, J.P., Pitcher, T.M., & Hay, D.A. (1999). Motor coordination and kinesthesis in boys with attention deficit-hyperactivity disorder. *Developmental Medicine and Child Neurology, 41,* 159-165.

Powers, M.D. (1989), What is autism? In M.D. Powers (Eds.), *Children with autism: A parent's guide* (pp. 1-29). Bethesda, MD: Woodbine House.

Pueschel, S.M. (2000). *A parent's guide to Down syndrome: Toward a brighter future.* Baltimore: Paul H. Brookes.

Rarick, G. L. (1980). Cognitive-motor relationships in the growing years. *Research Quarterly for Exercise and Sport, 51,* 174-192.

Reid, G., & Collier, D. (2002). Motor behavior and the autism spectrum disorders – introduction. *Palaestra, 18,* 20-27, 44.

Roberton, M.A. (1983). Changing motor patterns during childhood. In J. Thomas (Ed.), *Motor development during childhood and adolescence.* Minneapolis: Burgess.

References

Roberton, M.A. & Halverson, L.E. (1984). *Developing children: Their changing movement.* Philadelphia: Lea & Febiger.

Schalock, R.L. Luckasson, R.A., Shogren K.A., Borthwick-Duffy, S., Bradley, V., Buntinx, W.H.E., Coulter, D.L., Craig, E.M., Gomez, S.C., Lachapelle, Y., Reeve, A., Snell, M.E., Spreat, S., Tasse´, M.J., Thompson, J.R., Verdugo, M.A., Wehmeyer, M.L., & Yeager M.H. (2007). The Renaming of *Mental Retardation*: Understanding the change to the term *Intellectual Disability*. *Intellectual and Developmental Disabilities, 45*, 116–124.

Seefeldt, V. & Haubenstricker, J. (1982). Patterns, phases, or stages: An analytical model for the study of developmental movement. In J.A.S Kelso & J.E. Clark (Eds.), *The development of movement control and coordination.* New York: Wiley.

Seefeldt, V, Reuschlein, P., & Vogel, P. (1972). *Sequencing motor skills within the physical education curriculum.* Paper presented at the American Association for Health, Physical Education, and Recreation, Houston, TX.

Shapiro, B. (2001). Specific learning disabilities. In M.L. Batshaw (Ed.), *When your child has a disability* (revised) (pp. 373-390). Baltimore: Paul H. Brookes.

Sherrill, C. (2004). *Adapted Physical Activity, Recreation and Sport* (6th ed.). New York: McGraw Hill.

Sigman, M., & Capps, L. (1997). *Children with autism: A developmental perspective:* Cambridge, MA: Harvard University Press.

Slavoff, G. (1997). *Motor development in children with autism.* Unpublished doctoral dissertation. University of Virginia, Charlottesville.

Stewart, D., & Kluwin, T.N. (2002). *Teaching deaf and hard-of-hearing students: Content, strategies, and curriculum.* Needham Heights, MA: Allyn & Bacon.

Szapacs, C. (2006). Applied behavioral analysis *(ABA., Teaching Elementary Physical Education 17*(6), 12-15.

Thomas, J.R. (1997). Motor behavior. In J.D Massengale and R.A. Swanson (Eds.), *The history of exercise and sport science.* IL: Human Kinetics.

Thomas, J. R., Yan, J. H., & Stelmach, G. E. (2000). Movement characteristics change as a function of practice in children and adults. *Journal of Experimental Child Psychology, 75,* 228-244.

Towbin, K.E. (2001). Autism spectrum disorders. In M.L. Batshaw (Ed.), *When your child has a disability* (revised ed.) (pp. 341-353). Baltimore: Paul H. Brookes.

Wall, A. E. T. (2004). The developmental skill-learning gap hypothesis: Implications for children with movement difficulties. *Adapted Physical Activity Quarterly, 21,* 197-218.

References

Werry, J.S., Elkind, G.S., Reeves, J.C. (1987). Attention deficit, conduct, oppositional, and anxiety disorders in children. III. *Journal of Abnormal and Child Psychology, 15*, 409-428.

Winders, P.C. (1997). *Gross motor skills in children with Down syndrome: A guide for parents and professionals.* Bethesda, MD: Woodbine House.

Winnick, J., & Short, F. (1986). The influence on physical fitness test performance. *Journal of Visual Impairment and Blindness, 80*, 729-731.

Woolrich, D.L. (1994). *Attention deficit hyperactivity disorder.* Baltimore: Paul H. Brookes.

Yan, J.H., & Thomas, J.R. (2002). Arm movement control: Differences between children with and without attention deficit/hyperactivity disorder. *Research Quarterly for Exercise and Sport, 73*, 10-18.

Yan, J. H., Thomas, J. R. Stelmach, G. E., & Thomas, K. T. (2000). Developmental features of rapid aiming arm movements across the lifespan. *Journal of Motor Behavior, 32*, 121-140.

Yun, J., & Ulrich, D.A., (1997). Perceived and actual physical competence in children with mild mental retardation. *Adapted Physical Activity Quarterly, 14*, 285-297.

Zafeiriou, D.I. (2004). Primitive reflexes and postural reactions in the neural developmental examination. *Pediatric Neurology, 31*(1), 1-8.

Zelazo, P. D., Craik, F. I. M., & Booth, L. (2004). Executive function across the life span. *Acta Psychologica, 115*, 167-184.

Zelazo, N.A., Zelazo, P., Cohen, K.M., & Zelazo, P.D. (1993). Specificity of practice effects on elementary neuromotor patterns. *Developmental Psychology, 29*(4), 686-691.

Zhang, J. (2005). A quantitative analysis of motor developmental delays by adolescents with mild mental retardation. *Palaestra, 21*(1), 7-8.

INDEX

A

academic difficulties, 22
academic performance, 20, 22
accuracy, 12, 25
achievement, 7
activity level, 15
adaptation, 14
ADHD, 21, 22, 24, 25, 26, 27
adolescence, 37, 48
adolescents, 46, 50
adulthood, 13
adults, 46, 49
age, 1, 2, 5, 6, 8, 10, 11, 14, 18, 21, 22, 25, 27, 28, 30, 36, 43, 48
aggression, 29
aging, 15
aging process, 15
albinism, 34
alcohol, 4
alternative, 28, 32
American Psychiatric Association, 24, 27
American Psychological Association, 28, 45
antisocial behavior, 25
anxiety, 20, 22, 50
anxiety disorder, 22, 50
apraxia, 21
arithmetic, 18, 21
assessment, 11, 43
assessment tools, 43
athletes, 22
Attention Deficit Hyperactivity Disorder, 24
autism, 20, 27, 29, 30, 31, 32, 33, 45, 46, 48, 49
awareness, 23

B

behavior, ii, 3, 8, 18, 19, 20, 21, 26, 28, 31, 33, 48, 49
behavioral disorders, 20
birth, i, 4, 6
blindness, 20, 34, 35, 47
boredom, 20
boys, 10, 24, 25, 45, 48
Braille, 35
brain, 5, 6, 20
brain stem, 5
breast milk, 6
building blocks, 9

C

central nervous system, 5
cerebral palsy, 6
childhood, i, ii, 6, 14, 36, 37, 46, 48
children, i, ii, 1, 2, 6, 9, 11, 12, 14, 17, 18, 19, 20, 21, 22, 23, 24, 25, 26, 27, 29, 30, 31, 32, 33, 34, 36, 37, 38, 45, 46, 47, 48, 49, 50
classes, 1
classification, 18, 27, 47
closure, 32
coaches, 19, 20, 33, 43
coding, 27
communication, 27, 28, 29, 30, 32, 33, 36
communication skills, 30
community, 18
compensation, 4, 14
competence, 12, 50
components, 19, 37, 38
concrete, 19
conduct disorder, 24

confusion, 20
Congress, iv
control, i, 6, 7, 9, 18, 20, 23, 25, 30, 37, 45, 49, 50
control group, 6
cortex, 5
creep, 8, 36
cues, 14, 19, 23, 31, 32, 36, 37, 38, 39
culture, 13
curriculum, 23, 49

D

death, ii
decision making, 2
decisions, 11, 12
decoding, 21
deficit, 21, 45, 46, 48, 50
definition, 17, 34, 47
delinquency, 48
depression, 22
developmental disorder, 27
diabetic retinopathy, 34
diet, 4
disability, 17, 20, 21, 46, 47, 48, 49
discrimination, 21
disorder, 18, 21, 24, 25, 27, 36, 45, 46, 48, 50
diversity, 17
Down syndrome, 17, 18, 45, 48, 50
drug use, 25
dysgraphia, 21
dyslexia, 21, 22

E

ears, 33
Education, 1, 45, 46, 47, 49
educational programs, 11
endurance, 4, 14
environment, 4, 7, 9, 13, 14, 23, 25, 27, 30, 31, 33, 36, 38
environmental factors, 2
equilibrium, 6
excess stress, 4
execution, 13
exercise, 4, 14, 49
expertise, 13
exposure, 8

F

facial expression, 24, 28
fear, 36
feedback, 23, 37
feelings, 12
feet, 6, 9, 33
fetal alcohol syndrome, 18
fetus, 4
fitness, 11, 47
flexibility, 14, 18
flight, 10
focusing, 24, 34, 37
food, 33
football, 12, 22
frustration, 20

G

gait, 36
gender, 2
generation, 10
gestures, 28, 32
gifted, 20
girls, 10, 24
glasses, 34
glaucoma, 34
gold, 22
government, iv
growth, 1, 13, 46
growth spurt, 13
guidance, 23, 37
gymnastics, 13
gymnasts, 13

H

hands, 7, 8, 14, 29
House, 48, 50
human development, ii, 43
hyperactivity, 23, 24, 45, 46, 48, 50
hypothesis, 49

I

idiosyncratic, 28
imitation, 36
impairments, 22, 28, 34, 35, 36, 37, 38, 46, 47
impulsive, 24

impulsivity, 23, 24, 25
incidence, 21
independence, 7, 18, 38
indication, 6, 20
individual differences, 2, 4
individuals with Disabilities Education Improvement Act, 47
infancy, i, 5, 7, 9
infants, i, 6, 46
infection, 34
ingestion, 6
inhibition, 7
instruction, 3, 9, 10, 13, 14, 19, 23, 32
instructors, 26
intellectual disabilities, 17, 18, 19, 20
interaction, 4, 7, 9, 14, 23, 28
interactions, 5, 7, 28, 29
intervention, 36, 37

J

joints, 18

K

kinesthesis, 48
kinetics, 48
knees, 8

L

lack of confidence, 20
language, 21, 24, 28, 29, 32
later life, 9
LD score, 22
learners, 23
learning, 1, 3, 20, 21, 22, 23, 25, 31, 36, 45, 47, 48, 49
learning disabilities, 20, 22, 25, 45, 47, 48, 49
learning outcomes, 1
lesson plan, 1
life experiences, 12
life span, 50
lifespan, ii, 43, 48, 50
limitation, 18
long-term retention, 23
lying, i, 33

M

management, 26
manipulation, 6, 7, 30
mastery, 7, 23
maturation, i, ii, 10, 47
measures, 25, 30, 31, 34
memory, 18, 21
mental disorder, 28, 45
mental retardation, 17, 50
metaphor, 3, 4, 11, 14, 46
modeling, 38
momentum, 10
money, 18, 21
motion, 10, 32
motivation, 4, 24, 27, 31
motor behavior, i
motor skills, i, 3, 25, 30, 38, 49, 50
motor system, i
movement, i, ii, 2, 3, 4, 5, 7, 9, 10, 11, 12, 13, 14, 18, 23, 25, 35, 36, 37, 38, 46, 49, 50
muscle strength, i, 19
muscles, 6
music, 26, 33

N

neural development, 50
neuromotor, 50
neuroscience, i
normal aging, 14
normal development, 36, 43
nystagmus, 34

O

open spaces, 26
orientation, 37

P

pairing, 32
parents, 13, 29, 30, 36, 43, 47, 50
patellar tendon, 7
peer relationship, 28
peers, 2, 18, 19, 22, 24, 25, 29, 30, 33
performers, 12, 13, 14
physical activity, 14, 47

physical education, 11, 25, 31, 32, 35, 38, 43, 45, 46, 47, 49
physical fitness, 37, 46, 50
physiology, i
planning, 21, 22, 23, 38
population, 21
positive reinforcement, 26, 33
posture, 5
power, 10, 13
predictors, 6
preschool, 46
preschool children, 46
problem solving, 18
production, 5
psychology, i
puberty, 13

R

radio, 38
range, 24, 27, 29, 41
reading, 18, 20, 21, 22
reading comprehension, 21
reasoning, 21
reciprocity, 28, 36
recovery, 9
reflexes, 5, 6, 7, 50
regression, 14
rehabilitation, 43
reinforcement, 19, 33
relationship, 6
relationships, 48
resolution, 39
respiratory, 19
respiratory problems, 19
retardation, 47
rolling, 7, 33
routines, 28, 30, 33

S

safety, 38
sample, 30
school, 1, 20, 24, 43
search, 6
self-concept, 23
self-esteem, 22, 24
sensitivity, 30
severe intellectual disabilities, 18
severity, 27, 36
sharing, 29
shoulders, 10
sibling, 29
sign, 29
signs, 25, 32
skill acquisition, 4
skills, 9, 11, 13, 18, 23, 29, 30, 36, 37, 38, 45
smoke, 4
soccer, 19, 23, 32, 38
social development, 36
social impairment, 48
social skills, 27
special education, 21, 35
spectrum, 18, 27, 48, 49
speech, 5, 21, 28, 29, 41
speech sounds, 21
speed, 12, 14, 18, 21
spelling, 21
spin, 30
spinal cord, 14
spinal cord injury, 14
sports, 9, 11, 14
stability, 7
stages, 49
standard deviation, 18
standards, 18, 39
stimulus, 5, 6, 7
strabismus, 34
strategies, 18, 22, 23, 31, 37, 49
strength, i, 4, 6, 10, 13, 14
stretching, 32
stroke, 5
students, 1, 2, 22, 23, 26, 45, 48, 49
survival, 4
symmetry, 6
syndrome, 17, 18, 27, 48

T

targets, 27, 38, 39
teachers, 1, 19, 20, 33, 43, 45
teaching, 1, 11, 19, 22, 23, 25, 31, 37, 46
teaching strategies, 31
teens, 6
therapy, 33
thinking, 25
tonic, 6
toys, 29, 30
tracking, 43

transition, 26, 32

U

United States, 12

V

vacuum, 41
variability, 8
variables, 38
velocity, 10
vision, 34, 35, 37, 38
visual acuity, 34
visual environment, 31
visual field, 34, 35
visual processing, 22
volleyball, 12, 38, 39

W

walking, 5, 6, 7, 8, 9, 14, 17, 20, 30, 36, 39
wear, 30
withdrawal, 22
writing, 18, 21

Y

yield, 11, 43